Little People, **BIG DREAMS**™

SALLY RIDE

Written by
Maria Isabel Sánchez Vegara

Illustrated by
Alona Millgram

Frances Lincoln
Children's Books

Little Sally was a fearless girl from Los Angeles, California, eager to explore the world around her. Her parents always encouraged her and her sister to keep their minds and hearts open, reaching for the stars in everything they did.

Sally's love for science grew at school.
Solving math problems and tricky puzzles
felt like mental gymnastics to her.

Back home, she enjoyed playing with a chemistry set, looking at the stars with her telescope, and reading her favorite science magazine.

But Sally wasn't just smart, she was also a gifted tennis player. She was so good that it won her a scholarship to one of the best high schools in town. There, she met a very special teacher who inspired her to become a scientist.

DR. MOMMAERTS

NEWTONIAN MECHANICS
APPLIED PHYSICS
QUANTUM THEORY
THEORETICAL PHYSICS
ADVANCED PHYSICS

She was studying physics in college when she read that
NASA was looking for scientists to become astronauts.
More than 8,000 people applied, but only 35 were chosen.
Sally and five other women were part of that lucky group!

For five years, Sally learned parachuting, survival techniques, and everything there was to know about a space shuttle.

She even found time to earn her pilot's license and help
NASA build a gigantic robotic arm to use in space.

Her hard work and dedication paid off when Sally was chosen to join the space shuttle *Challenger* crew. She was about to make history as the first American woman to explore the universe beyond the bounds of Earth!

However, at that time, the press didn't take female astronauts seriously. They asked her many silly and sexist questions, like whether she cried at work. But Sally knew she was the right person for the job and kept working hard.

When the day finally arrived, Sally and her teammates felt
lonely as the hatch closed. Yet that feeling didn't last long.
Once they reached the atmosphere's edge and left Earth
far behind, the stars looked brighter than ever!

During their six-day mission, Sally did many scientific experiments and watched Earth from space. Looking back from above, she realized how precious and fragile our planet is and how humans must do all they can to protect it.

She was getting ready for her third mission to space when, sadly, seven fellow astronauts lost their lives in a shuttle explosion.

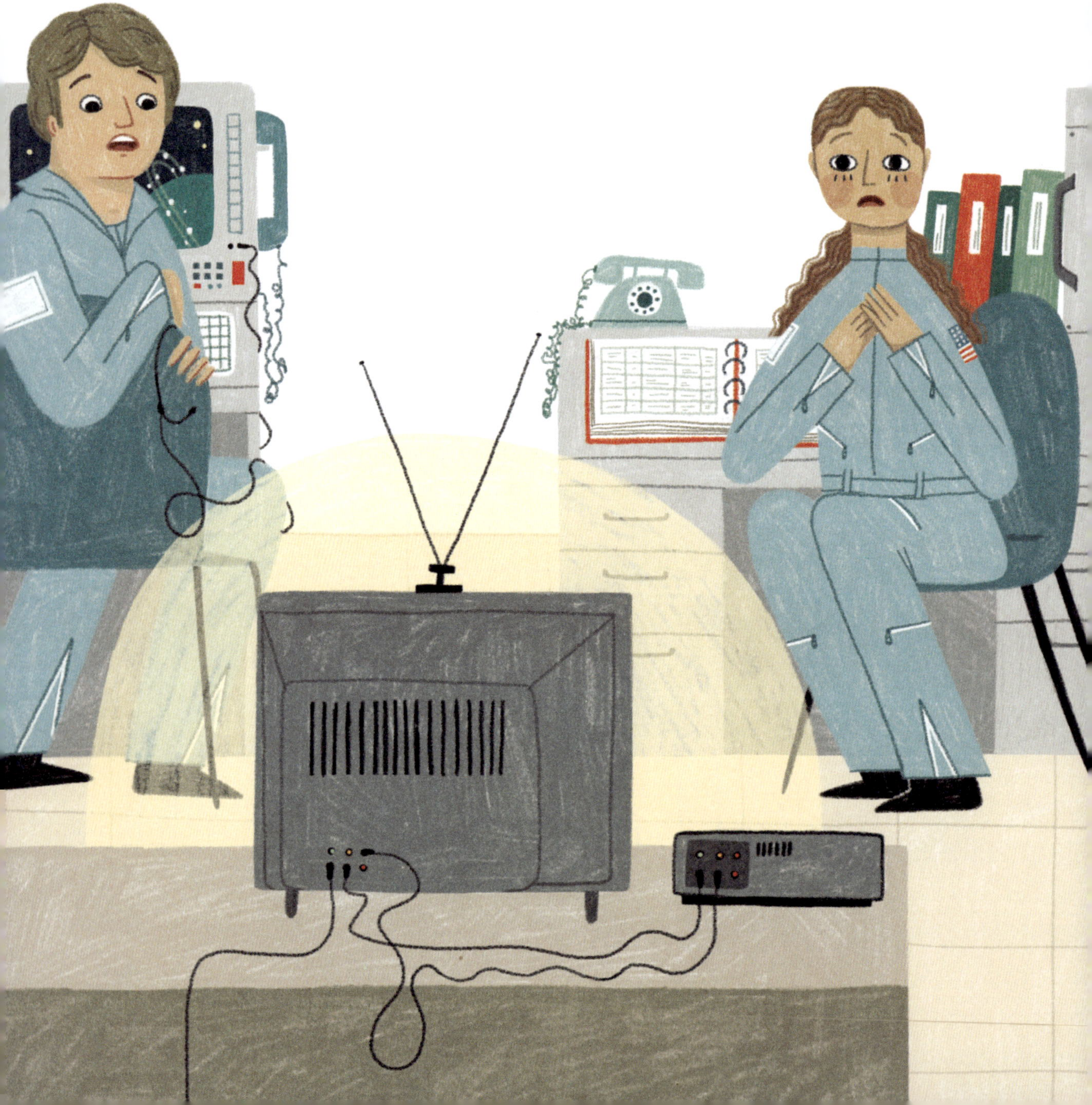

Sally helped to figure out what went wrong and gave
useful ideas so that it would never happen again.

After nine years as an astronaut, it was time for Sally to encourage others to follow in her footsteps. So, she became a physics professor and worked with NASA to set up a camera that allows students to take pictures of Earth from space.

Along with her partner, Tam, she started her own company: Sally Ride Science. Together, they wrote books for curious young minds and designed fun experiments to inspire children, especially girls, to get excited about science.

And the girl who believed there was something magical about learning, keeps inspiring us to discover the world.

That's why, as long as there are stars to reach for, there is
a place for little Sally in every young scientist's heart.

SALLY RIDE

(Born 1951 – Died 2012)

1978

1983

Sally Kristen Ride was born in Encino, California, seven years before the creation of NASA. Growing up, her parents encouraged her and her sister, Bear, to dream big and follow their interests. For Sally, this meant science and sports. She was a talented tennis player and as a teenager earned a national ranking. Off the court, she excelled at school and decided to study physics at Stanford University. While she was doing her PhD—a long research course—she responded to a NASA ad searching for scientists to become astronauts. It was the first time women could apply. Sally was selected and later made a mission specialist. Within a few years, she became the first woman to serve as a CAPCOM—the member of Mission Control who speaks to astronauts from the ground. Then it was Sally's turn

2003   2006

to leave Earth. In June, 1983, she boarded the space shuttle *Challenger* STS-7 as a flight engineer and became the first American woman to fly into space. Sally completed her second and final mission the following year. She was later appointed as the first director of NASA's Office of Exploration—an important role where she wrote a plan for America's future in space. After leaving NASA, she focused on bringing the joy of science to all children, but especially girls. She wrote many books, started Sally Ride Science, and helped teachers make their science lessons inspirational and inclusive. A year after she died, she was honored with the Presidential Medal of Freedom. Sally's story reminds us to seek adventure and follow our dreams: they may even lead us to outer space.

Want to find out more?
Have a read of this great book:

*How to be an Astronaut and Other Space Jobs: The Ultimate Guide
to Working in Space* by Dr Sheila Kanani and Sol Linero

Each June you can celebrate Sally's Night from anywhere in the world
https://airandspace.si.edu/sallys-night

Text © 2024 Maria Isabel Sánchez Vegara. Illustrations © 2024 Alona Millgram.
Original idea of the series by Maria Isabel Sánchez Vegara, published by Alba Editorial, S.L.U
"Little People, BIG DREAMS" and "Pequeña & Grande" are trademarks of
Alba Editorial S.L.U. and/or Beautifool Couple S.L.
First Published in the UK in 2024 by Frances Lincoln Children's Books, an imprint of The Quarto Group.
1 Triptych Place, London, SE1 9SH, United Kingdom. T 020 7700 6700 **www.Quarto.com**

A CIP record for this book is available from the Library of Congress.
ISBN 978-0-7112-9151-5
Set in Futura BT.

Published by Peter Marley · Designed by Lyli Feng
Commissioned by Lucy Menzies · Edited by Molly Mead
Production by Nikki Ingram

Manufactured In Guangdong, China CC102023
1 3 5 7 9 8 6 4 2

Photographic acknowledgments (pages 28-29, from left to right): 1. American astronaut and physicist Sally Ride (1951 – 2012)
watches a fellow pupil at Homestead Air Force Base, Florida, US, 31st July 1978 © Space Frontiers/Stringer via Getty Images.
2. Johnson Space Center, Houston, Texas: On board Scene-Astronaut Sally K. Ride, STS-7 mission specialist, communicates with
ground controllers from the flight deck of the Earth-orbiting Space Shuttle Challenger © Bettmann/Contributor via Getty Images.
3. Dr. Sally Ride speaks about the columbia tragedy at the San Diego Aerospace Museum February 7, 2003 © Sandy Huffaker/
Stringer via Getty Images. 4. Sally Ride, Ph.D, Recipient of the First-Ever California Hall of Fame and Governor Arnold
Schwarzenegger © Araya Doheny/Contributor via Getty Images.

Collect the *Little People,* **BIG DREAMS**™ series:

FRIDA KAHLO	COCO CHANEL	MAYA ANGELOU	AMELIA EARHART	AGATHA CHRISTIE	MARIE CURIE	ROSA PARKS	AUDREY HEPBURN

EMMELINE PANKHURST	ELLA FITZGERALD	ADA LOVELACE	JANE AUSTEN	GEORGIA O'KEEFFE	HARRIET TUBMAN	ANNE FRANK	MOTHER TERESA

JOSEPHINE BAKER	L. M. MONTGOMERY	JANE GOODALL	SIMONE DE BEAUVOIR	MUHAMMAD ALI	STEPHEN HAWKING	MARIA MONTESSORI	VIVIENNE WESTWOOD

MAHATMA GANDHI	DAVID BOWIE	WILMA RUDOLPH	DOLLY PARTON	BRUCE LEE	RUDOLF NUREYEV	ZAHA HADID	MARY SHELLEY

MARTIN LUTHER KING JR.	DAVID ATTENBOROUGH	ASTRID LINDGREN	EVONNE GOOLAGONG	BOB DYLAN	ALAN TURING	BILLIE JEAN KING	GRETA THUNBERG

JESSE OWENS	JEAN-MICHEL BASQUIAT	ARETHA FRANKLIN	CORAZON AQUINO	PELÉ	ERNEST SHACKLETON	STEVE JOBS	AYRTON SENNA

LOUISE BOURGEOIS	ELTON JOHN	JOHN LENNON	PRINCE	CHARLES DARWIN	CAPTAIN TOM MOORE	HANS CHRISTIAN ANDERSEN	STEVIE WONDER

MEGAN RAPINOE

MARY ANNING

MALALA YOUSAFZAI

ANDY WARHOL

RUPAUL

MICHELLE OBAMA

MINDY KALING

IRIS APFEL

ROSALIND FRANKLIN

RUTH BADER GINSBURG

MARILYN MONROE

KAMALA HARRIS

ALBERT EINSTEIN

CHARLES DICKENS

YOKO ONO

MICHAEL JORDAN

NELSON MANDELA

PABLO PICASSO

AMANDA GORMAN

GLORIA STEINEM

FLORENCE NIGHTINGALE

HARRY HOUDINI

J.R.R. TOLKIEN

ELVIS PRESLEY

NEIL ARMSTRONG

ALEXANDER VON HUMBOLDT

NIKOLA TESLA

WILMA MANKILLER

MARCUS RASHFORD

LAVERNE COX

MAE JEMISON

DWAYNE JOHNSON

HELEN KELLER

ANNA PAVLOVA

QUEEN ELIZABETH

TERRY FOX

HEDY LAMARR

SHAKIRA

FREDDIE MERCURY

LEWIS HAMILTON

LOUIS PASTEUR

PRINCESS DIANA

DAVID HOCKNEY

VANESSA NAKATE

OLIVE MORRIS

KING CHARLES

MOZART

STEVE IRWIN

JÜRGEN KLOPP

LEO MESSI

SALLY RIDE

TENZING NORGAY

Scan the QR code for free activity sheets, teachers' notes and more information about the series at www.littlepeoplebigdreams.com